Memories of Aberdeen

(A facsimile reproduction)

Printed by The Acorn Press, Carnoustie

Copyright 1988

ISBN 1 870978 03 X

Keith Murray Publications
46 Portal Crescent, Tillydrone
Aberdeen, AB2 2SP

INTRODUCTION

Louisa Innes Lumsden was born in 1839 into an affluent Aberdeen family. As an adult she travelled widely and concerned herself with most of the social issues of her time, in particular the women's suffrage movement and anti-vivisection. In later life she was honoured by St. Andrews University and also received the O.B.E.

"Memories of Aberdeen" reflects and comments on the values and lifestyle of what was then a distinct and largely self-contained social class. In the narrative which follows the treatment is characterised by a refreshing honesty and the book has captured the life and atmosphere of an age of gentility which has forever disappeared.

K.M., F.C. and J.R.W.
1988

Memories of Aberdeen

A Hundred Years Ago

LOUISA INNES LUMSDEN

From 'St Leonards School, 1877-1927'
(Oxford University Press)

Memories of Aberdeen

A Hundred Years Ago

Edited by

LOUISA INNES LUMSDEN, D.B.E., LL.D.

Second Edition, Enlarged

ABERDEEN: WILLIAM SMITH & SONS
THE BON-ACCORD PRESS
1927

MEMORIES OF ABERDEEN

A Hundred Years Ago

ANY winters ago, when snow lay deep on the hills around our home in the country and shut out the world, my sister Katharine had the happy inspiration to ask my Mother to speak of her early days, and to preserve her reminiscences in writing, and since then the few who have read these memories have often told me that they should be published. I trust, therefore, that they may have an interest at any rate for Aberdonians. It is a very simple chronicle—the things remembered by a happy young woman in the early years of the last century, memories of travelling by coach or with post-horses from stage to stage, of hospitable inns where sumptuous breakfasts in the morning and abundant dinners in the afternoon awaited the guests, of a northern city where the county people had town-houses and

spent gay winters, and of sociable country visit-
ings—a picture of quiet, pleasant days when
nobody was in a hurry.[1]

My Mother was the third daughter of James
Forbes, a merchant in Aberdeen, of the family
of Forbes of Watertoune, a cadet branch of
Tolquhoun. Watertoune was sold in 1770 to
George, Earl of Aberdeen. The ruins of the
old house still stand, a mere fragment, on the
wooded banks of the Ythan near the town of
Ellon, and the old Castle of Tolquhoun, more
distant, is fast falling into decay. Echt, now
called Dunecht, was built by James Forbes, his
father, William Forbes, having bought the estate.
He was anxious to recover Watertoune, but
Lord Aberdeen declined to sell. There was no
house on Echt, the old residence was House-
dale, and there William Forbes and his wife
lived. She was a daughter of a physician in
Montrose, the Honourable Thomas Arbuthnott,
brother of the 6th Viscount, and of his wife,
Elizabeth Forbes of Thornton. My Mother often
stayed as a child at Housedale, and remembered her grandmother, Elizabeth Arbuthnott,

---

1. It seems strange that in these reminiscences of troubled and
stormy times, there is, just as in Jane Austen's novels, not a word about
war, but I have heard my Mother speak of Paul Jones and the fear he
inspired. The people in Aberdeenshire used to say that Bonaparte
would " sup his Yule sowens " at the wells of Pannanich on Deeside.

very distinctly—a stately little lady with beautiful reddish hair, dressed in winter in grey silk, in summer in white muslin. Every morning after breakfast she would go to the farm to see her dairy, then to the brew-house where the strong ale and home-brewed beer used in the household were made, and then to her garden which she loved. She made quantities of rosewater and *pot-pourri*, the last of which, even still fragrant, I burned only some twenty years ago. The dinner-hour at Housedale was 4 o'clock, the house was always full of friends and their washing was done for them—quantities of white dresses, petticoats, etc. The spinning-wheel was still in use and servants span a good deal. They wore wrappers in the morning, put on white aprons in the afternoon and wore gowns only on Sundays.

My Mother was born in 1807 at Springhill, a pretty little place about three miles from Aberdeen, where the family lived in summer; in winter they lived in the house on Trinity Quay, then one of the fashionable parts of the town, and went to the country in the second week in April after the Church week. She and her two elder sisters had a governess, Miss Urquhart, a very nice woman, the daughter of Dr. Urquhart of Nairn, and when in 1815 their father took them to school in Bath (the long journey was made with post-horses), Miss Urquhart stayed on for two years, and after she left my Mother used to ride into Aberdeen to have lessons. Her father had no carriage; he rode into Aberdeen daily to business. Everybody went about on horseback; my Mother remembered her uncle, her mother's brother, Sir Harry Niven Lumsden, and her aunt, Miss Rachel Niven, afterwards the wife of Captain Carmichael, riding about paying visits, a servant, also of course mounted, behind, carrying their things in saddle-bags.

Women were employed on farms to cut the corn with sickles; it was great praise to say of a woman that she was " a good heuker," but hay was cut with a scythe. The last sheaf of corn, called the Cliack, was kept tied up with blue ribbon and usually presented to one of the girls, my Mother or her sisters.[1] They opened the ball in the barn afterwards.

One of my Mother's earliest reminiscences was of a crowd of people, mostly women, passing the gate of Springhill, returning from Aberdeen. They were in great excitement, having just been

---

1. An older custom observed in some parts of Aberdeenshire was to bring the Cliack home dressed as a maiden, put it over the door for a night and then give it to the best cow. Is there in this curious custom a relic of human sacrifice, a thank-offering for harvest?

to see a lad of sixteen or seventeen hanged for sheep-stealing. A man had been apprehended at the same time as the boy, and the two were being taken to prison in a cart, when the man sprang out, jumped over the bridge across the Denburn in Union Street, and was killed. There was great indignation among the people on account of this execution and the cruelty of the law.

Smuggling was common, and whisky-stills were often hidden among the hills. At Echt, where, after the death of his father at House-dale, my grandfather lived, my Mother, out walking one day, met people coming from Aberdeen with three empty carts. They had gone into town, carrying, apparently, wooden things for sale at the "Timmer Market," but in reality kegs of whisky hidden underneath, and having sold the whisky, they were returning in triumph with pipes playing and flags flying, and in this style they had marched past the door of the ex-ciseman, Malcolm Gillespie,[1] who lived at Skene. He was so enraged that he afterwards kept watch for them, and after a great fight at Bridge-end, near Waterton, brought two of the smugglers, with bandaged and bloody heads, to

1. Gillespie was executed for forgery and arson. *Historical Aberdeen*, p. 72, by G. M. Fraser.

Echt, to get a warrant from my grandfather to
take them to Aberdeen. It was too late to send
them away that night so they had to be kept in
the house.

My grandmother Forbes laid the foundation
stone of the house of Echt. It stood on high
ground with heather all around, and my Mother
remembered seeing the whin and broom burning
when the approaches were laid out. The work
was done chiefly by Highlanders who spoke
Gaelic.

My grandfather's family were Whigs and
Presbyterians, but his wife, Jane Niven, was an
Episcopalian. Her father, John Niven, had
been, as a boy, in prison with his father at
Carlisle after the Rebellion in the " Forty-five,"
and to the end of his life he was a strong Jacobite
and non-juror, as well as a devoted member of the
Scottish Episcopal Church. He was a rich man,
having made a fortune in the tobacco trade (like
the "tobacco lords," the leading merchants in
Glasgow). When my Mother's eldest sister,
Rachel, was to be baptised, a great difficulty
arose. One grandfather would not go to a
christening in church, and the other refused to
come to one at home. At last a compromise
was arranged. Mr. Skinner, afterwards Bishop
of Aberdeen (the son of the Rev. John Skinner,

the author of *Tullochgorum*), who was the clergy-man of the Scottish Episcopal Church, at that time only a room in Long Acre, agreed to baptise the baby at home, and the Episcopalian grandfather, following his example for they were great friends, was willing, after all, to be present.

Mr. Niven's brother-in-law and friend, Mr. Gordon of Craigmyle, a most benevolent and kind-hearted man, had, strangely enough, a mania for attending executions, and would even go on the fatal platform with the criminal. Among the many old letters which I have had to burn was one from him to his friend, filling four pages of the old-fashioned square sheets of paper, and containing nothing except warm expressions of affection and reflections upon the blessings of the Lord's Day—it was written on a Sunday.

Mr. Niven was twice married. His first wife, Rachel Lumsden, was my Mother's grand-mother. Her brother, Harry, had been a planter in Jamaica. He bought Clova from John Lumsden of Cushnie, and lived and died there— the people about the place used to speak of him as "Kingston Harry." It is said that a cask of Madeira stood in the hall at Clova and everybody could draw from it as they pleased. He did not like the marriages of his two elder sisters, and left Clova to the son of his youngest sister, Mrs. Niven, who, on succeeding to the estate, took the name of Lumsden. Mr. Niven's second wife was one of three sisters, heiresses; the other two were Mrs. Henderson of Caskieben, and Mrs. Young, the wife of Provost William Young of Sheddocksley. The daughter of this second marriage, Catherine, married a Yorkshire man, John M. His father, who had a large property, took a dislike to the boy, and sent him when he was about eight years old to Aberdeen, to be boarded with a heckler (brushmaker) in the Hardgate, and brought up to the man's trade. Time passed ; the boy's uncle, General M., came home, asked what had become of his nephew, and hearing that there was an Episcopal church in Aberdeen, wrote to Bishop Skinner, begging him to find out the boy and have him properly boarded and educated at his expense. The Bishop and Mr. Niven were intimate friends, and thus young John came to visit in Mr. Niven's house. When he was old enough, his mother's brother, Sir Robert Calder, who was in the Navy, took him to sea, and when he returned to Aberdeen to see his friends, he fell in love with my Mother's aunt, Catherine Niven, and asked her to marry him. Her father, however, would not agree to the marriage until my

Mother's uncle, Sir Harry Niven Lumsden, went
to England and made inquiries about the young
man's parentage, when, satisfactory information
having been obtained, the marriage took place,
but the old father refused to give his son any-
thing. Young John M. left the Navy, and they
lived at Elsick very happily, but constantly in
debt, and Mr. Niven and Sir Harry Lumsden
had to pay the bills. It was a delightful house
to visit in, and my Mother was very fond of
them both. They had three children, and were
afterwards joined by a younger brother and
sister, who had quarrelled with their father and
left home. One Sunday morning in autumn,
they were all going to church, and John was to
ride. His horse reared and threw him, and a
few days afterwards he died. His widow, my
Mother's aunt, left Elsick and lived at Rose-
mount near Gilcomston. Her sister, who afterwards married Mr. Fraser of Williamston, lived
with her and another brother, Henry, who also
had been turned out of doors by his father.
Later she succeeded to Glassel left her by her
mother's aunt, Mrs. Young, and lived there.
Her son, John, was educated by his uncle,
General M., and sent to Cambridge, and while
he was there his grandfather died, and he
succeeded to the estate. A story is told of

old Mrs. Young that once when Mr. George Douglas was staying with her at Glassel, they began one evening to read *The Mysteries of Udolpho*, and were so entranced by the book that they read on until the maid came in the morning to open the shutters.

In 1824, my Mother, like her sisters, was sent to school in Bath, and her father and mother, her sister, Elizabeth, and a cousin, Harry Mackenzie, the son of my Mother's favourite sister, Christina, the wife of Roderick Mackenzie of Glack, went with her. They were five days at sea in the smack *Nimrod*, and this was considered a very good passage. There was no stewardess, and they were all sea-sick, but after a little while, lying under an awning spread over the deck, they got quite well and enjoyed the voyage. A lace merchant was the only passenger my Mother remembered, and he told her mother all his history. She was of such a sympathising nature that, wherever she went, somebody poured out his troubles to her. She was very handsome, with a very sweet face and beautiful dark eyes.

They arrived in London on a Sunday morning, and the town was so full that they had difficulty in finding rooms in any hotel, but finally settled in the Osborne, a grand hotel in

the Adelphi, where they had the rooms in which
the King and Queen of the Sandwich Islands
had stayed. They had a delightful time in
London, drove out every day in what was called
a glass coach with a pair of horses, saw the
Tower and other sights, went to Vauxhall, then
very fashionable and beautiful, "a blaze of light,"
and one evening went to the theatre to see
Ellison acting *Tartuffe*. Then came the journey
to Bath. They left by the coach at 6 a.m.,
breakfasted at Maidenhead, dined at Marl-
borough, and reached Bath in the evening.

Two years were passed at Mrs. Penson s
school. The Christmas and Easter holidays
were spent in Bath with Colonel and Mrs.
Shaw, old family friends. Edith Richardson,
afterwards Mrs. Shaw, and my Mother were
school-fellows, having been together at Mrs. Bell
Gordon's school in Queen Street. It was by the
advice of her brother, Captain John Clements,
that Mrs. Richardson sent her daughter to
Aberdeen to be under the care of his cousin,
Mrs. Lumsden, of whose sense and judgment
he had the highest opinion. When the Mid-
summer holidays came, Mrs. Penson took her
four Scottish girls — my Mother, a Kerr, a
Gordon, and a Lumsden, to Cheltenham and
Clifton, then very fashionable places. Leghorn

hats were the fashion, and my Mother must have looked charming in a white muslin dress, lavender silk spencer, and a broad Leghorn hat trimmed with lavender ribbon and wheat-ears. That summer, 1826, the weather was unusually warm and there was a great drought. At Clifton the water-carts went about selling water, and in Scotland the crops failed—they were so short in some places that they were gathered with the hand.

While at school my Mother sometimes spent a day with Aberdeenshire friends, who were then living in Bath—the three Miss Grants of Monymusk, and Major and Mrs. Mitchell, she was Miss Forbes of Newe. Mrs. Mitchell was the best and kindest of women and spoke the broadest Scots. One evening they took my Mother to the theatre, and Mrs. Mitchell, who was very tall, talked in a very loud voice, and was dressed in a red silk gown, red turban and coral ornaments, must have been a conspicuous figure. When she and Major Mitchell, whom she always called the "Mawjor," went out driving, their servants, black Tom and black Sally, sat behind in the rumble.

School days over, my Mother returned to Aberdeen, as she had gone to England, by sea. She left London with her brother John on a

Sunday morning in June. They had very great difficulty in getting a carriage to take them to the wharf, and when at last they reached it the ship was gone. On this they got into a wherry, gave the boatman a sovereign and caught the ship, the *Bon-Accord*, at Blackwall. They were ten days at sea, provisions ran short, even the water was done, and a boat had to be sent to Cromer for supplies. Among the passengers was an Aberdeenshire couple, Mr. and Mrs. A. B., who had a hamper of provisions and enjoyed their good things on deck, but gave nothing to the poor sick people below, and my Mother was so disgusted with this behaviour that she refused to dine with them and preferred the rough dinner in the cabin. They were so long at sea that the *Bon-Accord* was given up for lost.

Soon after my Mother came home, she went to Edinburgh with her parents and her sister Edith, who had come home from school in bad health, and was taken to Edinburgh to consult a doctor. They drove from Echt to Stonehaven, where they breakfasted ; at Perth they dined and slept in the Salutation Inn, and reached Edinburgh next day in the late afternoon, when they went to what was then thought to be the best hotel, the British Hotel in Queen Street.

They went by the Carse of Gowrie and came back by the Vale of Strathmore. Poor Edith was ordered by the doctor never to sit, but always to stand or lie down. Probably had she been more wisely treated she might have recovered. She died in 1831. Another sister, Maria, had already died in Bath in 1829, and a third, Christina, died at home in 1833, all three, it would seem, from the cold of Bath, and foolish fashions in dress. My Mother's school-fellow, Jessie Anne Gordon, the daughter of Mr. Francis Gordon of Craig who lived in Golden Square, died also of consumption at school. Girls at school had to wear low dresses even in winter, and the only neck covering allowed was a coral necklace, to which the poor creatures clung as their only comfort. Low white muslin dresses with long white cambric gloves were worn winter and summer at Miss Giroux's dancing school, and my Mother's evening dress was a crimson poplin, with long, dark kid gloves to keep her arms warm.

Dress, wise or foolish, sanitary or the reverse, seems to have been an even more important matter in those days than in ours. Scattered notices of it in my Mother's reminiscences tell of her elder sisters wearing in winter crimson cloth pelisses and sealskin caps with gold bands and tassels, or puce silk pelisses and Highland bonnets with plumes of black feathers. Her mother had a velvet pelisse, brown, but when rubbed the wrong way gold colour (surely it was plush, not velvet); and her aunts, Joan and Anne Forbes, wore in winter crimson velvet pelisses, white muslin skirts and silk stockings and shoes. Did people ever go out in rain or snow in those days, and was the weather less treacherous?

Country fashions were, however, still very simple. The only bonnets, or rather hats, to be seen in the Parish Church of Echt were in the laird's pew. The older women wore tartan plaids or red cloaks and mutches—a hideous headgear—and the girls had only snoods binding their hair.

Modern comforts were sadly lacking, but no doubt not missed. Gas and water had not yet been brought into Aberdeen. Some houses had cisterns on the roof for rain water, and in every house there was what was called a "stand," a sort of hand-barrow with a cask, to which an iron can was attached, for carrying water from the wells. This stand was set under the pump, and the maid-servants gathered of an evening round the wells, enjoying a gossip before carrying the water home. The wells were built of stone, the best were thought to be in Golden

Square and Belmont Street ; all the water for
the houses on the Quay was carried from the
well in the Shiprow. The mineral Spa Well
had still a considerable reputation for its curative
properties. Matches had not then been invented.
Spunks was the name given to them at first,
later lucifers. In country houses, and very likely
in town houses too, the kitchen fire was carefully
dumped down every night to make sure of light
in the morning.

Union Street and Union Terrace were only
partly built, and people were gradually moving
up from the Green, Marischal Street, the Quay,
Exchequer Row, and other old parts of the town
to Union Street, Golden Square, and Belmont
Street. General Hay had a fine house in the
Upperkirkgate, and my Mother's grandfather,
John Niven, one in the Guestrow, which he
called Thornton Court, after a small property
which he had near Keith Hall. It is a beautiful
old house, built by Sir George Skene in 1669,
and in it the Duke of Cumberland lodged for
six weeks on his way to Culloden. It is now,
I believe, the Victoria Lodging House.[1] The

1. Guestrow, really Ghaistrow. It overlooked the town church-
yard, and was supposed to be the scene of the nightly walks of the
ghosts of the dead. The Victoria Lodging House. *Historical Aberdeen*, by G. M. Fraser.

houses in Albyn Place, in the first of which Sir Charles Bannerman lived and after him the Miss Cumines, were considered to be quite in the country, and Provost Gavin Hadden with his family lived in the Green in winter and at Union Grove in summer. The beautiful old Cross of Aberdeen stood on the edge of the Plainstaines in the Castlegate. Readers of *The Antiquary* will remember Mrs. Shortcake's praise of Lovel: "That Lovel dings a' that ever set foot on the plainstaines o' Fairport." Gentlemen used to walk up and down on the plainstaines, ladies never. What, one wonders, was the origin of this taboo? All the principal shops were in Broad Street, Lyall's (now in Union Street), Baillie Stewart's, who was succeeded by his nephew, Mr. Walter Stewart, and the shop of Mr. Jamieson, the jeweller. Mr. Glegg, the confectioner, had a shop in the Shiprow. Miss Bain was the leading confectioner, but where her shop was my Mother did not say.

About this time my Mother's uncle, Mr. Forbes Robertson, who took the name of Robertson on succeeding to Hazlehead, left him by Mr. Robertson, was adding to the house, probably the present front which hides the older and more picturesque part behind.

Among early friends in the country, my

Mother remembered old Mr. Skene of Rubislaw, Sir Walter Scott's friend, who lived at Skene House. He was the nearest neighbour to Echt and often dined there. He was a great lover of dogs, and when he died left money to keep them and their tombs. My grandfather's second cousin, Mr. George Douglas (of the Tilquhillie family) and his cousin, Miss Harriet Ferguson, would often ride over to Echt from Maryfield on Deeside to breakfast, and so, too, would Hugh and Charles Irvine, the sons of old Mr. Irvine of Drum. The dinner hour at Echt in summer was 5 o'clock, there was tea at 6, and at 7 the girls would go out to ride. Surely these rides tell of a different climate from what we have now—of hot summer days when outdoor exercise would be taken in the cool hours of the early morning or late evening. Another neighbour was Sir Thomas Burnett of Crathes— one of four brothers, each of whom in turn succeeded. He died in London, and when my Mother's brother, William Forbes, went to see him when he was dying, he found the garden before the house all sown with thistles to remind Sir Thomas of Scotland and his beautiful home on Deeside.

One of my Mother's pleasantest recollections of her girlhood was a round of visits paid with

her father and mother and her sister, Rachel, in
Kincardineshire and Forfarshire. They went
in the carriage, the coachman, as usual, riding
postillion, and as there happened to be a race
meeting at Montrose they stopped there for it.
After the races, and before the ball in the evening, there was an Ordinary—what would be
called now a *table d'hôte*, at which, of course,
they all dined, but the two girls were unwilling
to go to the ball, as they had no proper ball
dresses and only black shoes. However, to the
ball they went, enjoyed it thoroughly, and
danced the whole night. A rope was stretched
across the ball room—how odd this sounds in
our days!—and on one side the county danced,
on the other the town. My Mother danced one
dance on the town side with the brother of her
English governess at school. Most of the evening she danced with young Marmaduke Ramsay,
a Fellow of Oxford. The Ramsays were then
still at Fasque.

The winters in Aberdeen were very gay.
The fashionable dinner hour was 5.30, later
6 o'clock. Children had an early dinner, but
there was no set luncheon, only some slight
refreshment for their elders and cake and wine
for visitors. An evening party with dancing
generally followed the dinner. For a party of

about sixteen the dinner would be two soups, two fish dishes, a joint and a top dish, two side dishes, *e.g.*, turkey and tongue, and four corner dishes, all on the table. Vegetables were handed round. An épergne stood in the centre, but there was no other decoration. After the evening party there would be a light supper, surely light after such a dinner!

One of the most delightful balls my Mother remembered was given by Lady Innes of Edengight in a small house in Silver Street. Miss Betty Gordon of Leicheston gave one great party every year, and it was thought a very distinguished gathering. She and old Mrs. Lumsden were great genealogists and had long talks together on this, to them, very interesting subject. General Hay gave many parties in the Upperkirkgate, and Mrs. Henry Lumsden and Mrs. Peter Farquharson of Whitehouse in Union Terrace. Mrs. Peter Farquharson was an eccentric character. On one occasion Mrs. Carmichael was entertaining a large party when Mrs. Peter entered, apparently in high dudgeon, but in reality enjoying the joke, and announced to the company that she had just heard the town crier, bell in hand, proclaiming to the crowd the loss of " Mistress Peter Farquharson's wig!" One winter when Miss

Foote, the actress, came to Aberdeen, Mrs. Peter took seats in the Shakespeare box, but when she arrived she found the seats already occupied. She desired the intruder, Mr. Leslie Cruickshank, to leave, but he objected—he could not, his wife was with him. "Tak' her wi' ye," said Mrs. Peter, and she sent for Mr. Ryder to settle the dispute. He came, dressed as he was for the stage, and the end of it was that Mr. and Mrs. Leslie Cruickshank had to climb over the front of the box into the pit, which that night was arranged like the boxes. Mrs. Peter was triumphant, and long afterwards her first question on meeting any of her friends was, "Ken ye ane Leslie Cruickshank?"

Races were held every year in Aberdeen. My Mother was taken as a child to one race-meeting at which the Duke of Gordon, Duke Alexander, and his son the Marquis of Huntly, afterwards Duke George,

"Cock o' the North, my Huntly braw,"

had each a horse running, and the son's horse, "Bonnie Jamie," beat the Duke's horse, "Teddy the Grinder." Mrs. Boswell of Kingcausie, a very beautiful young woman, was on the grandstand, and my Mother, who was charmed by her beauty, had brought a bunch of carnations for her. Mrs. Henry Lumsden asked for some, but the child would not spare any from Mrs. Boswell. "Little," said my Mother, "did I think that she was to be my sister-in-law."

There were four assemblies every winter; they began at 9 and ended at 12, when the band played "Gude nicht and joy be wi' ye a'." The dances were country dances, waltzes, reels and quadrilles. One autumn there was a great race-meeting and they all went into Aberdeen for it. There were races on three days, and every day an Ordinary at 5 o'clock in the County Rooms (now the Music Hall Buildings). The company met in the large ballroom, then the folding doors were thrown open, and they went into the banqueting room. The Ordinary dinners cost a guinea, the tickets for the grand stand about 5/-, and the ball tickets were extra.

The ball began at 9 o'clock, General John Ramsay took charge and called the dances, and my Mother danced the first country dance after supper with him. There were no pipers for the reels. Supper followed, at which there were toasts and songs and speeches, and gentlemen asked ladies to take wine with them. Dresses were short to the ankle and narrow. My Mother and her sisters wore at this great meeting white tulle dresses trimmed with silver over white satin, white satin shoes, and long kid gloves. Their hair was dressed in large bows and curls. After the races, and before the Ordinary, gentlemen came to call. One can imagine the bows and curtseys which accompanied the calls, as in a scene from one of Miss Austen's novels, *Emma* or *Pride and Prejudice*.

One winter, perhaps it was in 1831, there was a great snowstorm. Nine mails were due in Aberdeen. There was no snow-plough at Echt—perhaps snow-ploughs had not yet been invented. It was a man's daily work to bring supplies to the house from the farm. The coals were all kept for my grandmother's fire, as she was ill, and the wood was all done. At last the road was cut and they got into Aberdeen.

A very strange story among my Mother's reminiscences is worth telling, though the connection with her own life is only very slight, showing as it does the rigour of law a hundred years ago, like the story of the poor boy who was hanged for sheep-stealing. A young friend of the family, De Winter Moir, who came to Aberdeen to stay with his guardian, Mr. Moir of Scotstown, and was often at Echt, had a brother, Major Moir, who was hanged for what was called murder. He lived on the bank of the Thames, and the bargemen were in the habit of taking a short cut across his grounds, which annoyed him greatly and he tried to stop them. One day he and a man came to high words, and the same day at dinner he heard that the man was again on his ground. He took his gun and went out to turn the intruder away, and again there were high words. The man raised his stick to strike, and Major Moir, who was a first-rate shot, fired at his elbow, intending only to disable him and protect himself. The wound was not serious, though a bone was broken, but being neglected or mismanaged in the hospital to which the man was taken, mortification set in, and he died about a week afterwards. Major Moir was tried for murder, convicted, and sentenced to be hanged. The case was manifestly a desperately hard one, and there can be no doubt that he would not have been hanged had he not been a gentleman. But the Government had been hanging men all round for incendiarism and rioting, and they did not dare to let him off. There was great excitement about it, for Major Moir was well known and very popular, and thousands went to see him hanged, the people saying they were sure "the Major would die game!"

My Mother was married on the 3rd July, 1827, at Echt House. Both her brothers, William, who was at Oxford, and John, who was in business in London, came down for the wedding. My Father was Clements Lumsden (so named after his mother's cousin, Captain John Clements, R.N.), the youngest son of Harry Lumsden, advocate in Aberdeen, and his wife, Catherine McVeagh. Her father, Hugh McVeagh, son of Ferdinand McVeagh of Drewstown, Co. Meath, having in true "agin the Government" Irish fashion got into political hot water and been obliged to leave Ireland, drifted to Aberdeenshire, started a linen manufactory at Huntly (his mother was one of the Richardsons of Belfast, linen manufacturers), and married Catherine Lumsden, daughter of the Laird of Cushnie. They had two daughters, of whom one married her cousin, Harry Lumsden, and the other, Margaret, married Lewis Farquharson, chief of the Inverey branch of the Farquharsons. Mrs. Lumsden did not altogether like her sister's marriage, as Lewis Farquharson was poor and a Roman Catholic. After the marriage they went to Ireland, he hoping, no doubt, to mend his fortunes there, but he got mixed up in political troubles, so finally they went to Canada, and several years passed away before they returned to

Scotland. Then his cousin, Lewis Innes of Ballogie, who had no heir, his son and brother being
both priests, sent for him, and on Lewis Innes's
death in 1815 he succeeded to Ballogie. It was
for this reason that he and his son Lewis dropped
the name Farquharson and were called Innes.
His daughter, Eliza Farquharson, died un-
married; another, Louisa, married Luke Nether-
ville Barron, Surgeon in the Royal Scots
Regiment. They lived in the Correction Wynd
in Aberdeen, and in summer, first at Balnacraig,
later at Ballogie.

At the wedding of my Father and Mother
white gloves, as the fashion then was, were
given to all the guests, to married ladies short
white gloves, to young ladies long ones which
cost 3/6 the pair. Altogether the expense of
the gloves for the wedding came to £50. Bride
and bridegroom stayed for the dinner, and at
dessert a magnum of claret, bottled when the
bride was born, was on the table. The same
thing was done when my Mother's sister, Rachel,
was married in 1832 to Patrick Carnegy of
Lour, and when her brother William was born,
their grandmother poured a bottle of claret over
the baby, no doubt for luck. As everybody
knows, claret was to the Scots what port was in
those days to the English :

"Let him drink port, the English statesman cried,
He drank the poison and his spirit died."

For the first winter after their marriage my parents lived with the old people, who in the winter lived in 1 Union Terrace and in the summer at Belhelvie Lodge. Old Mrs. Lumsden, as Kitty McVeagh, born and brought up at Huntly, had many stories to tell my Mother of her young days there. She was a great favourite with the Duchess of Gordon, the famous Duchess Jane, who lived at Huntly Lodge, and raised the 92nd Gordon Highlanders in 1796. The Duchess prided herself on her knowledge of "braid Scots," and once, when someone, trying to puzzle her, begged to know what "a gowp o' glaur" meant, she promptly replied, "a nievefu' o' clairts," a handful of mud. No domestic detail was beneath her notice, and when one day a fishwife demanded to see her, and would sell her fish to nobody else, she readily talked with the woman and in the end, after long bargaining about prices, had to give in and the greedy fishwife was victorious. Great was the laughter when it turned out that the pretended fishwife was no other than the Marquis of Huntly, who was very triumphant over his success in bamboozling his mother.

My grandmother, herself the proud mother

of five tall sons, and in whose eyes daughters were the signs of a decadent family, could not control her disappointment when my sister Katharine was born. "Lord be here," she exclaimed, "anither lassie!" She was a very outspoken person, and once with dire results. Her man servant, Thomas, brought a visitor upstairs, placed her behind the draught-screen drawn across the door and announced Mrs. ——, and Mrs. Lumsden instantly called out, "Dinna let her in, Tammas, I never could thole Kirsty Jamieson!" "She's here, ma'am," calmly said Thomas, whereupon the unwelcome visitor emerged from behind the screen, and we may be sure both ladies civilly ignored the unlucky fact, one that she had spoken and the other that she had heard the hasty words.

When my parents set up house for themselves their first servants were a cook, maid, housemaid, and a boy as footman. The cook's wages were £8 a year and £2 for tea money, and the housemaid had £6 and £2 for tea. The dinner hour was 5 o'clock. The best meat, prime joints, cost 6d. the lb., a sheep's head 6d. But the quartern loaf cost 9d., sugar 1/- the lb., and tea 6/6, or 8/- for a finer quality. Fish was very cheap. A whole cod could be got for 1/-, large haddocks for 2d., and a dozen whitings for 6d. The fish-wife would sometimes give 13, a fisher's dozen as it was called. The fishwives sat with their creels on the steps of the Cross. Aunt Carmichael used to send quantities of Findon (Finnan) haddocks to the Duke of Gordon in London. They were great friends. She used to tell how clever the Duke was in blowing out a candle without leaving a spark in the wick—a difficult feat with the candle of those days, a tallow dip.

Among the winter gaieties in Aberdeen were fancy balls, and my Mother went to her first fancy ball as Diana Vernon, in what, it must be confessed, was a very odd costume for the part, a black satin dress, tartan scarf, and a Highland bonnet with white feathers. My Father, who had been one of the Celtic Guard of Honour, raised by Sir Walter Scott when George IV. came to Edinburgh, wore his Highland dress.

At another fancy ball Lewis Innes went as an Eskimo, but afterwards he put on his Highland dress. He had left his bonnet on a bench while he was dancing, and Farquharson of Finzean, who had got rather tipsy, snatched it up and pulled out the eagle's feather. There was a great disturbance and nearly a fight, but my Father succeeded in restoring peace.[1]

In the summer of 1833 my Father and Mother went abroad. They crossed to Antwerp, and after five days in Brussels, went on by diligence to Liége, Namur, and Aix-la-Chapelle, then up the Rhine to Cologne, Coblentz, and Frankfurt. From Frankfurt they hurried back to Paris to be in time for the Three Days, the anniversary of Louis Philippe's accession. They left Frankfurt on Wednesday afternoon, stopped only for a short rest and food at Metz and Saarbrück, and reached Paris about three on Sunday morning. In Paris they stayed at the Hotel des Princes in the Rue Richelieu, where they had beautiful rooms. There were fêtes and fireworks, and a great review in the Place Vendôme. Louis Philippe and his two sons, the Dukes of Orleans and Nemours, were present on horseback, and the other boys with the Queen on a balcony.

Another summer my Mother went with her mother and sisters to the Bridge of Earn, near the Pitcaithly Wells. The Hotel was full of guests, mostly friends from Aberdeenshire and Forfar-

---

1. Farquharson pedigree and claims to chiefship. *Balmoral in Former Times*, pp. 15 *et seq.*, by the Rev. John Stirton, D.D.

shire, and the Count de Damas and other members of the suite of Charles X., who was then occupying the rooms in Holyrood which had sheltered him as Comte d'Artois in 1775. The party made excursions every day to Scone, Kinfauns, and Moncrieff House, and once, standing on Moncrieff Hill, they talked about a tunnel being made under it, and laughed at such a thing being thought possible.

My Father, with Admiral Henderson and Mr. Newell Burnett, went to Bridge of Earn to fetch my Mother, and they came home by Blairgowrie and Braemar, where the great sight was the Linn of Dee.

My Mother died on the 19th December, 1883, and I may conclude these brief reminiscences with one of the many tributes of respect and affection paid to her memory. It came from an old servant, Mrs. Mackay. "She was a noble lady, so upright and so downright and so straightforward."

" Kindness, brightness, truthfulness, these were the qualities that impressed themselves on everybody who knew her."

With these words, written by my sister, Katharine, the little book ends from which I have drawn a few memories of a hundred years ago.

PRINTED BY WILLIAM SMITH & SONS
AT THE BON-ACCORD PRESS
ABERDEEN

MRS CLEMENTS LUMSDEN
(Jane Forbes)
Circa 1870

KATHERINE MARIA LUMSDEN

Hon. Superintendent Aberdeen H.S.C. 1885-1892
Hon. Secretary Aberdeen District Nursing Association
1892 for *circa* twenty years.

LOUISA INNES LUMSDEN
D.B.E., M.A. Cantab., Hon. LL.D. St Andrews

From 'St Leonards School, 1877-1927'
(Oxford University Press)

Poems

by

Louisa Innes Lumsden

HITCHIN

Reprinted from 'Beautiful Britain Series — Girton College.'

AYE, here's the place. You recollect
That Sunday, don't you, long ago?
We rested here. Slant struck and low
The westering sun, the grass was fleck'd

Thro' blossoming linden branches sweet
    With chequer'd lights. Even now, the same,
    And see, the scarlet poppies flame
Still, 'mid the swaying, springing wheat.

Then, too, as now, wild roses flung
    Their fragrant breath to breezes cool
    From delicate-veinëd cups brimful
Of dew, and dark-leafed ivy clung

About the hedge, or twined and crept
    Around the gnarled elm-boles. How clear
    It seems still after many a year,
That picture! Dim the shadows slept

On yonder heights, a dusky blue,
    But Offley Woods seemed all ablaze
    In the low sunshine. As I gaze
How I recall it all! And you?

No need to speak! I see your eyes
    Fixed yonder on the far-off hill,
    And mine somehow are dim — but still
I know that in the hollow lies,

Beyond the lanes, beyond the Park,
    The quaint old town, its market square,
    Its gabled roofs, unchanged are there,
But ah! how changed that house we mark,

Or only fancy we discern,
    Dull red, upon the green hillside;
    I know 'tis there, and crimson dyed
The westward fronting windows burn,

As in the pleasant years bygone,
  When we were fellow students there;
  I wonder, were those days as fair
As memory paints, now years have flown?

Why prove and test the vanish'd Past?
  Sweet are the memories it leaves —
  Faint as the scent of violets — sheaves
Of garnered knowledge too amassed —

Oh, trifling, doubtless! Yet that gain
  Suffices, we're content; we'd give,
  Would we not, ah! how much, to live
Our college life all o'er again!

The work, the energy, the power,
  The strenuous effort, the content,
  The gladness effort brought well spent,
The freedom of an idle hour,

When laugh and song went round, or talk
  In graver mood, or merry play,
  Game or charade, or, ere the day
Died o'er the woods, a random walk.

You're tired, I talk too long; we'll go,
  Dine at the 'Sun,' then take the train
  For Cambridge — this way, by the lane —
We've two hours still to spare or so —

Then on to Girton. But for me,
  My memories cling to Hitchin still,
  To yon red house upon the hill,
To every field, to every tree,

'Twas here I mused, 'twas here I read,
  Here learned the worth of friendship, here
  Felt the world widen round, saw clear
Horizons stretch, and overhead

A bluer sky. For here I came
  Sick to the soul for larger scope,
  Glad labour, self-expression, hope,
All the girl's life denied of aim

And new life granted. Can I tell
  My gain? Ah, here, one moment, wait —
  We catch a glimpse still. No, too late,
Old College, from us both, farewell!

SPRING

('Alma Mater's Mirror,' St Andrews University, 1887.)

WHAT though the winds of March be rude,
   And though the air be chill,
The touch of Spring is on the wood,
   Her breath is on the hill.

She bids yon throstle pipe so clear
   Amid the woodland ways;
She leads the shivering trembling year
   Toward the sweet summer days.

O wondrous Spring!   O golden hour,
   Whence is thy crown of blessing?
Lo! this is thy transcendent dower —
   All hoping, nought possessing.

And therefore is it, O fair Spring,
   With wealth of incompleteness,
My dumb soul hath no voice to sing
   According with thy sweetness.

For my sad heart, in sorrow pent,
   Doth iron Winter hold;
And all my thought is backward bent
   To the dear days of old.

YONDER (*ÈKEÎ*).

SUNSHINE steeping the heather,
  And a wind in the pines astir,
My friend and I wandering together
  Long ago, in the days that were.

Or lying in sunshine golden
'Mid the heather warm and sweet,
In those bygone summers olden,
  He crouching close at my feet.

Then nearer beside me he'd nestle,
  Where my hand might stroke his head
But awatch for the faintest rustle,
  Or the lightest word I said.

While the curlew, circling and swooping,
  Whistled around us shrill,
And down on the breeze came stooping
  The hawk from the windy hill.

Ah me! my friend, he was only
  A doggie, but he was dear,
And since he went — oh! how lonely
  Seem all the moorlands here.

Fleet-footed, unweary, white-breasted,
  Watchful by day and night,
With eyes that on me still rested
  Loving, and full of light;

Brown eyes — ah! sightless and clouded
  Ere thy little span was o'er,
And now, O my darling! shrouded,
  Earth-hidden for evermore.

Nay, we know not.   Howe'er we ponder,
  That riddle remains unread,
What things may await us yonder
  Where are those we call the Dead.

Thou dead!   Nay, surely far rather
  In some higher life elsewhere;
And I trust our all-loving Father
  To meet thee and know thee there.